## Learning About Landforms

# Islands

Ellen Labrecque

Raintree is an imprint of Capstone Global Library Limited, a company incorporated in England and Wales having its registered office at 7 Pilgrim Street, London, EC4V 6LB – Registered company number: 6695582

www.raintreepublishers.co.uk
myorders@raintreepublishers.co.uk

Edited by Rebecca Rissman, Daniel Nunn and Catherine Veitch
Designed by Steve Mead
Picture research by Elizabeth Alexander
Production by Victoria Fitzgerald
Originated by Capstone Global Library
Printed and bound in China

ISBN 978 1 4062 7224 6
17 16 15 14 13
10 9 8 7 6 5 4 3 2 1

**British Library Cataloguing in Publication Data**
A full catalogue record for this book is available from the British Library.

**Acknowledgements**
We would like to thank the following for permission to reproduce photographs: Alamy pp. 8 (© Travel Pictures), 20 (© Emmanuel LATTES); Getty Images pp. 9 (Torsten Blackwood/AFP), 11 (Michael Dunning/Photographer's Choice), 13 (PARK YEONG-CHEOL/AFP), 14 (Bob Stefko/Photodisc), 15 (Viviane Ponti/Lonely Planet Images), 17 (Patrick AVENTURIER/GAMMA), 18 (© Laszlo Podor/Flickr), 19 (Popperfoto); naturepl.com pp. 22 (© Doug Allan), 29 (© Aflo); Science Photo Library p. 10 (Christian Darkin); Shutterstock pp. 4 (© photobank.kiev.ua), 5 (© Tatiana Popova), 12 (© Igor Plotnikov), 16 (© SUPACHART), 21 (© Konstantin Stepanenko), 23 (© Steffen Foerster), 24 (© Pierre Leclerc), 25 (© Subbotina Anna), 26 (© Deborah Kolb), 27 (© Aleksandar Todorovic), 28 (© Laborant); SuperStock p. 6 (Planet Observer/Universal Images Group).

Cover photograph of Parata Headland and Sanguinaires Islands reproduced with permission of Corbis (© Marc Dozier/Hemis).

Every effort has been made to contact copyright holders of material reproduced in this book. Any omissions will be rectified in subsequent printings if notice is given to the publisher.

# Contents

Some words are shown in bold, **like this**. You can find out what they mean by looking in the glossary.

# What are landforms?

Look around when you are outside. You may see mountains, hills, valleys, caves or islands. Earth is made of these natural landforms. This book is about islands.

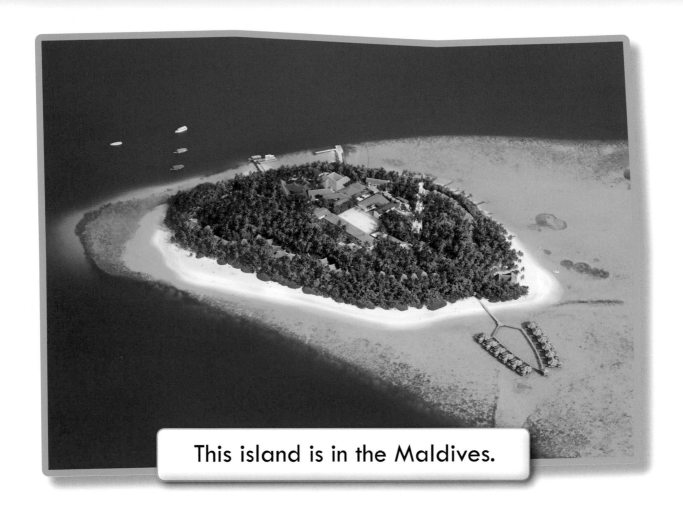

This island is in the Maldives.

Earth is always changing. Earth's landforms are made in different ways over millions of years. Some islands are made from volcanoes. Others are made when large areas of land split and move over time.

# What are islands?

Islands are land surrounded on all sides by water. Islands are found in oceans, rivers, lakes or ponds. Islands are different sizes. Greenland is the world's largest island (about 2,175,000 square kilometres).

Greenland

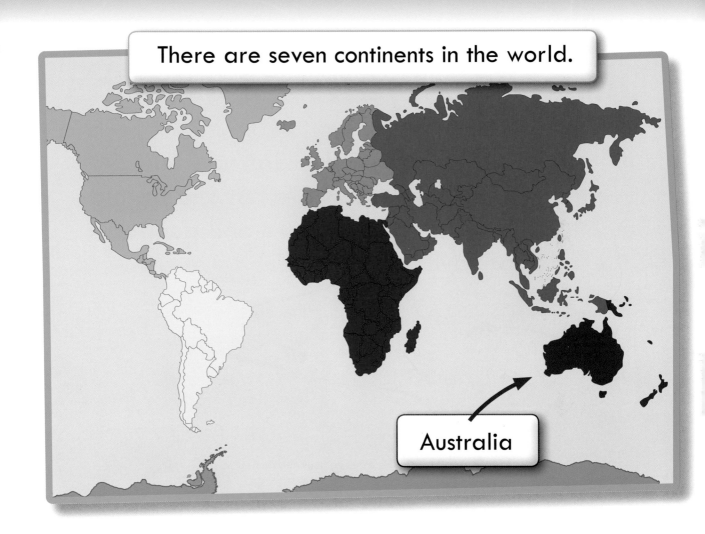

There are seven continents in the world.

Australia

Australia is surrounded on all sides by water, but Australia is not an island. Australia is too big to be an island (about 7,741,220 square kilometres). Australia is a **continent**. Continents are much bigger than islands.

# Different types of islands

Islands can be different. Some are cold and covered in ice. Other islands are hot and **humid**. Some islands have lots of animals and people. Others do not have many.

This island is heart-shaped. It is called Lovers' Island.

Manukan Island,
Malaysia

Islands are made in different ways. There are six types of islands. These are continental, tidal, barrier, coral, volcanic and artificial.

# Continental islands

Continental islands were once part of a **continent**. Scientists think that millions of years ago, there was only one large continent on Earth. Over time, this continent broke into pieces. Some of these pieces became continental islands.

All the countries on Earth were once joined together in one massive continent called Pangaea.

Great Britain
is a continental
island.

Continental islands are also made when the sea
floods over land and cuts off other parts of land.
The British Isles were made into an island in this
way. The British Isles were once part of Europe.

# Tidal islands

Tidal islands are types of continental islands. They are still joined by land to the **mainland,** but the join is under water most of the time.

Mont Saint-Michel is a tidal island in France.

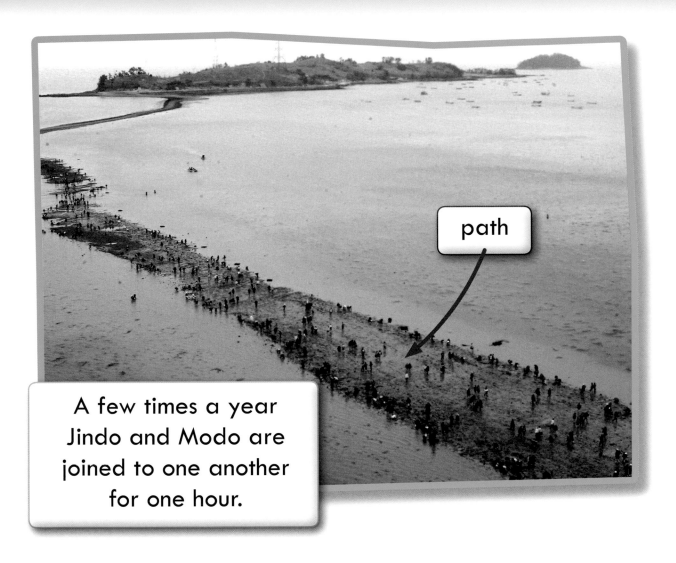

path

A few times a year Jindo and Modo are joined to one another for one hour.

Jindo and Modo are two tidal islands near South Korea. A few times a year, the sea level goes down and a path opens up between the two islands.

# Barrier islands

Barrier islands are made when the sea piles up sand into **sandbars**. The sandbars rise above the seawater and make islands. Barrier islands lie next to coastlines. They protect the coastline from storms, waves and wind.

Padre Island in Texas is the world's longest barrier island.

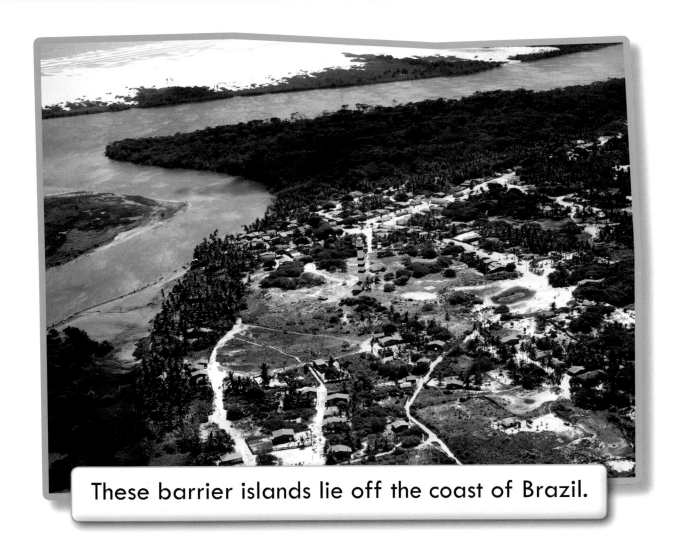

These barrier islands lie off the coast of Brazil.

Many barrier islands were also made during the most recent **ice age** (11,700 years ago).

# Coral islands

Coral islands are made of billions of tiny **exoskeletons**, or dead animals' bones. Other materials, like rock and sand, mix with the coral. This helps the island grow big and rise from the bottom of the sea.

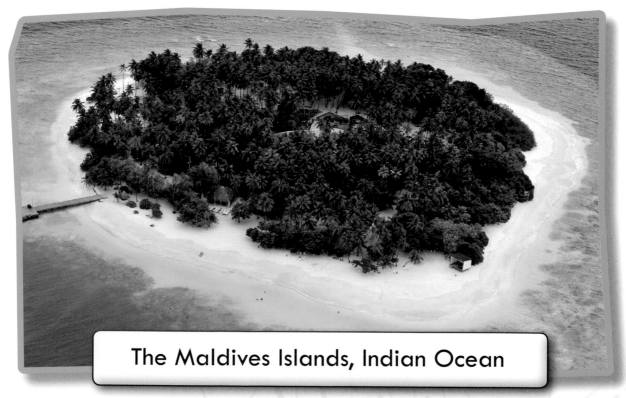

The Maldives Islands, Indian Ocean

Tuvalu Islands, South Pacific

The storms that create coral islands can also damage and destroy them. Waves attack one side and dump material on the other.

# Volcanic islands

When an underwater volcano **erupts, lava** flows out and down the sides of the volcano. The lava cools and piles up. When the volcano grows big enough, it rises above the water and forms an island.

The Hawaiian Islands are volcanic islands.

Scientists study the new plant and animal life on Surtsey Island.

In 1963, Surtsey Island was created when a volcanic eruption spewed hot lava into the Atlantic Ocean near Iceland.

# Artificial islands

Artificial islands are another type of island. They are not really landforms, because people created them. Hundreds of years ago on Lake Titicaca, the Uros people made islands out of **reeds**, off the coast of Peru.

Homes and boats on Lake Titicaca are also made from reeds.

This artificial island is shaped like a palm tree.

In Dubai in the United Arab Emirates, people have created islands shaped like palm trees and a map of the world. The islands are made out of sand. The sand has been moved from the Persian Gulf and sprayed into shapes near the shore.

# Island animals

Different animals live on islands. The animals that live on continental islands are similar to the creatures that live on the nearby **mainland.**

This walrus lives in Greenland.

Creatures swim
or fly to volcanic
islands from all
over the world.
Animals are also
carried to volcanic
islands on floating
plants that have
been swept out
to sea.

This blue-footed
booby lives on the
Galapagos Islands.

# Plants and trees

Some islands are home to beautiful plants. Some plant seeds arrived on islands by drifting in the ocean. Coconut tree seeds are enclosed in hard shells that can float a long time. The seeds of red mangrove trees often float to new places, too, along a coastline.

bird of paradise flower, Hawaii

Seeds can also travel to islands by wind, and birds can carry seeds to islands. The seeds get stuck on the birds' feet or feathers, or they get tucked in their droppings!

# Island people

Many scientists say the first people to live on the islands in the Pacific Ocean came from Southeast Asia. These people sailed in canoes across the sea around 3,000 or 4,000 years ago. They were called Polynesians.

These Polynesians live on an island in the Pacific Ocean.

Java, Indonesia

Today, millions of people live on islands. Java in Indonesia is the world's most crowded island. More than 100 million people live there.

# Islands today

Many people love islands, especially **tropical** or warm ones. People love to swim, dive and play on island beaches.

But islands are also at risk from rising sea levels and fierce weather such as **tsunamis** and hurricanes. Scientists study ways of saving islands. They hope to make a difference, so we can always enjoy islands.

# Glossary

**continent**  one of seven of the largest landmasses on Earth

**erupt**  explode or break open

**exoskeleton**  hard outer shell that protects some animals

**humid**  hot and sticky

**ice age**  period of time when large sheets of ice covered large areas of land

**lava**  hot, melted rock that comes out of a volcano

**mainland**  big area of land

**reeds**  tall, stiff grass that grows on or near water

**sandbar**  exposed or underwater ridge of sand built by waves offshore

**tropical**  weather that is hot and sticky

**tsunami**  destructive sea wave caused by an underwater earthquake

# Find out more

**Books to read**

*Geography Now: Islands Around the World,*
    Jen Green (Wayland, 2012)
*Investigate Geography: Landforms,* Jane Penrose
    (Heinemann Library, 2010)
*Landform Adventures: Ocean Divers,* Anita Ganeri
    (Raintree Publishers, 2012)

**Websites to visit**
**www.bbc.co.uk/nature/humanplanetexplorer**
A great place to explore islands and our world.

**kids.nationalgeographic.com/kids**
Type "islands" into the search box to find all kinds
of information about islands.

**www.worldatlas.com**
Explore maps and landforms on this site.

# Index